Young Learner's
PICTURE DICTIONARY

Words:

Alison Niblo
and
Janet De Saulles

Consultant: Betty Root

Pictures:

Kim Woolley

Contents

Note to the reader

Action words, such as **walking**, are printed in gray.
These words tell you about what is happening in the pictures.

McGraw-Hill
Children's Publishing

Pets

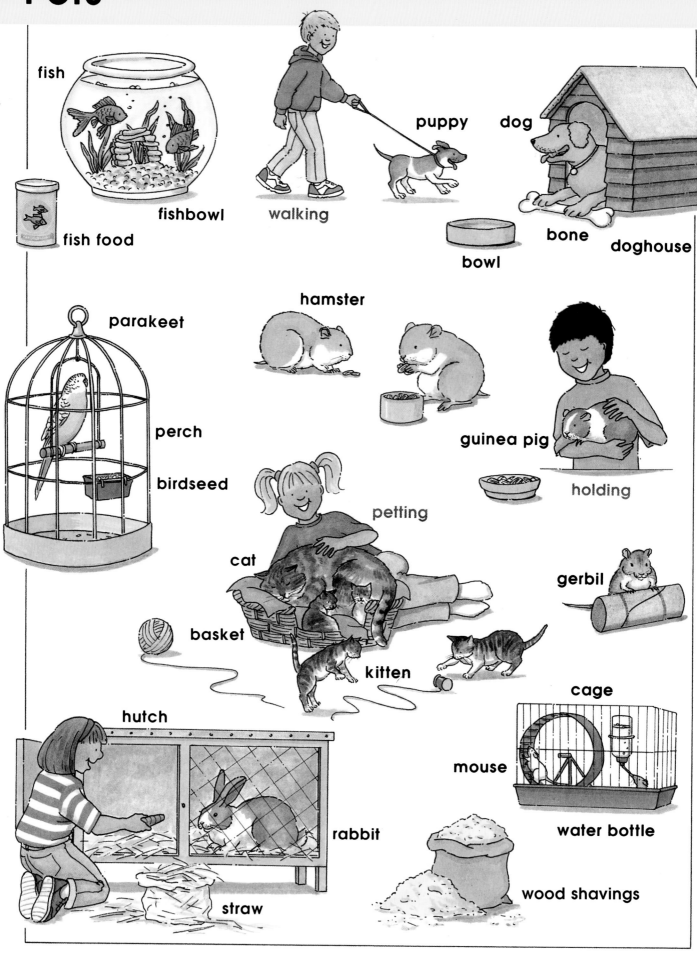

fish

fishbowl

fish food

walking

puppy

dog

bone

doghouse

bowl

parakeet

perch

birdseed

hamster

guinea pig

holding

petting

cat

basket

kitten

gerbil

cage

mouse

water bottle

wood shavings

hutch

rabbit

straw

Insects

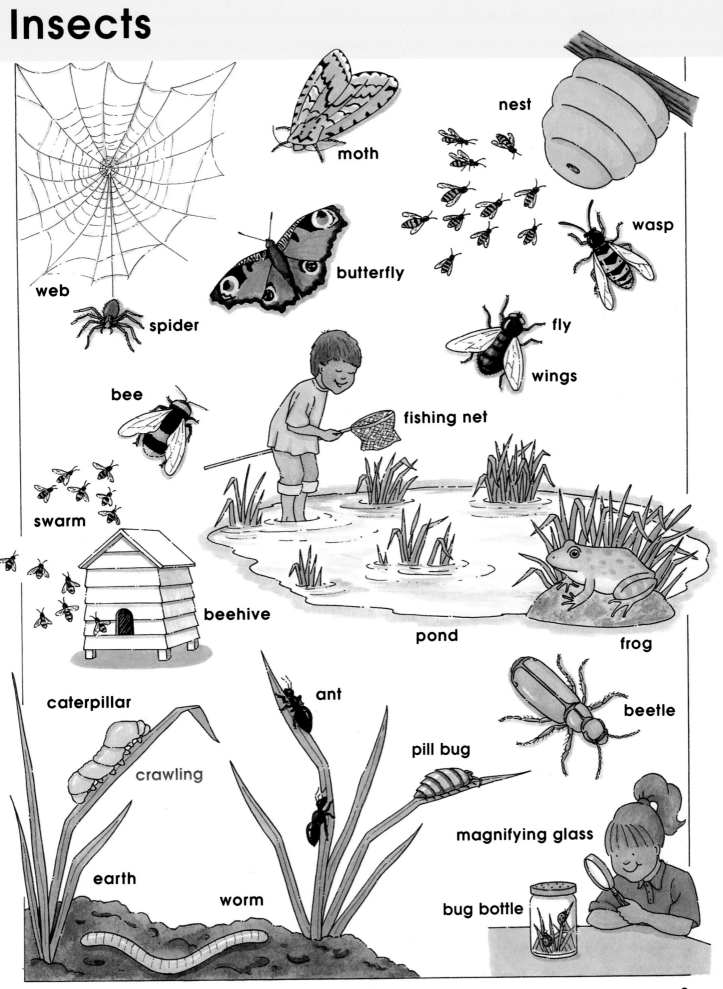

web

moth

nest

wasp

butterfly

spider

fly

wings

bee

fishing net

swarm

beehive

pond

frog

caterpillar

ant

beetle

crawling

pill bug

magnifying glass

earth

worm

bug bottle

At the zoo

monkey

scratching

elephant

gorilla

rhinoceros

giraffe

zebra

tiger

cheetah

running

lion

dolphin

kangaroo

snake

polar bear

shark

penguin

seal

octopus

turtle

crocodile

hippopotamus

eel

pool

4

In the country

woods

hill

truck

combine

sheep

lamb

farm

field

barn

stable

gate

horse

pigpen

farmer

hen

tractor

pig

orchard

bull

goose

hedge

duck

cow

duck pond

stream

Fun outdoors

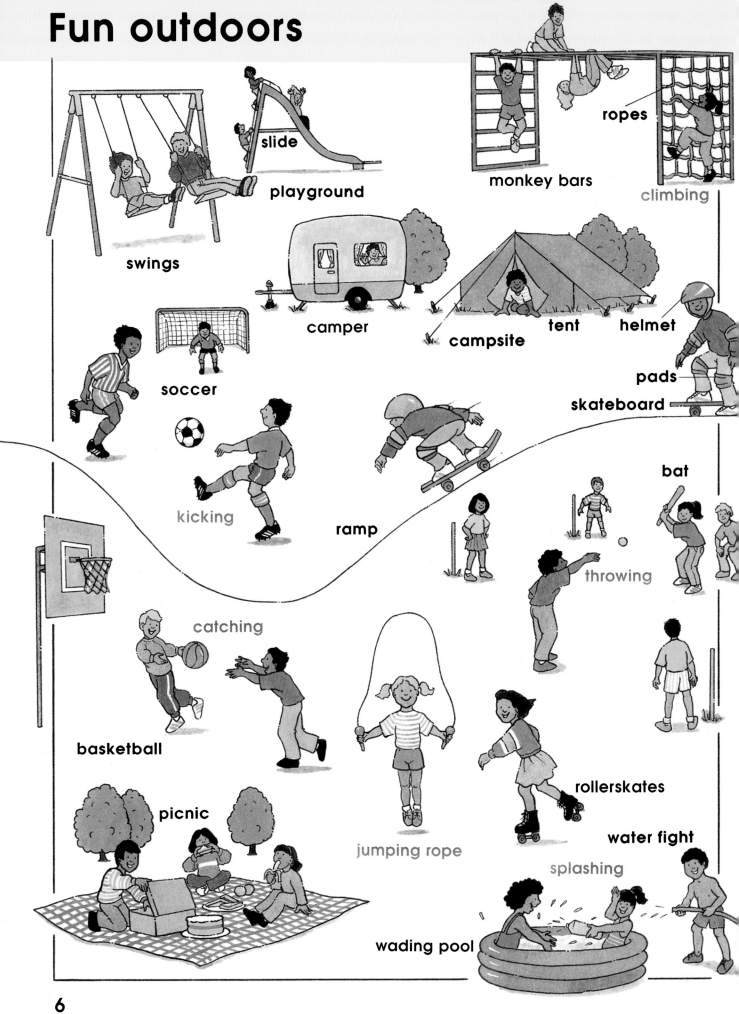

slide

playground

swings

ropes

monkey bars

climbing

camper

tent

helmet

campsite

pads

skateboard

soccer

kicking

ramp

bat

throwing

basketball

catching

rollerskates

picnic

jumping rope

water fight

splashing

wading pool

6

At the amusement park

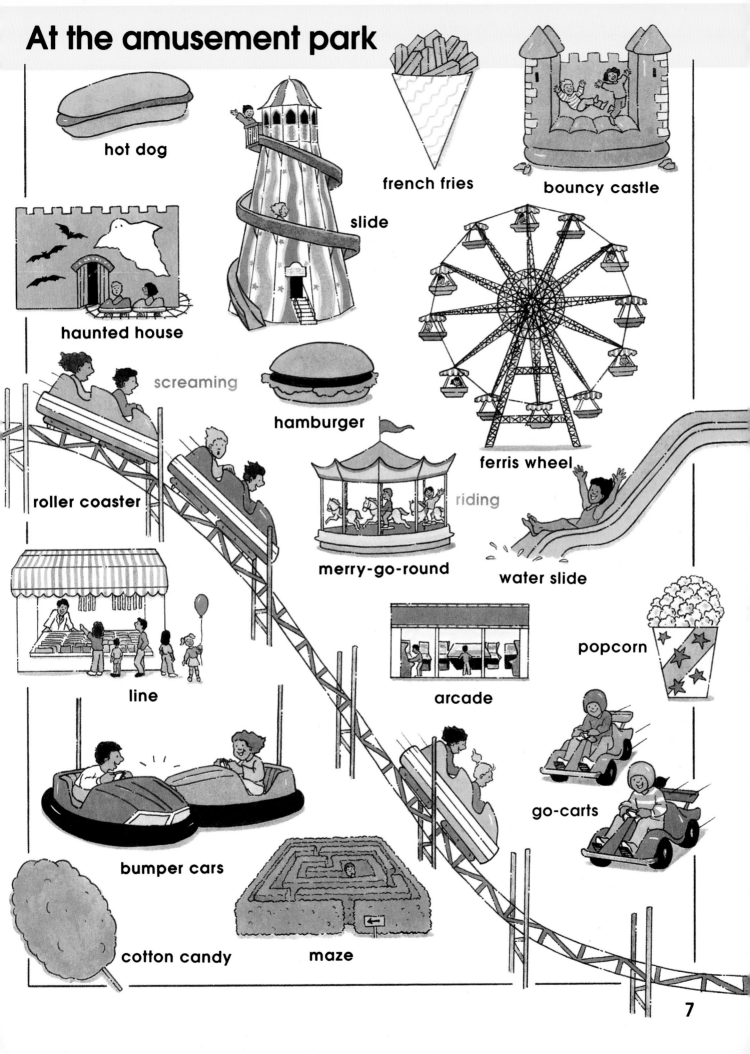

hot dog

french fries

bouncy castle

slide

haunted house

screaming

hamburger

ferris wheel

roller coaster

riding

merry-go-round

water slide

line

arcade

popcorn

bumper cars

go-carts

cotton candy

maze

At the beach

ice cream

bowling game

goggles

snorkel

ice cream stand

beach mat

wet suit

pier

crab

flippers

starfish

lifeguard

water skiing

seaweed

wading

inner tube

water wings

digging

shovel

making

moat

bucket

sand

pebbles

sandcastle

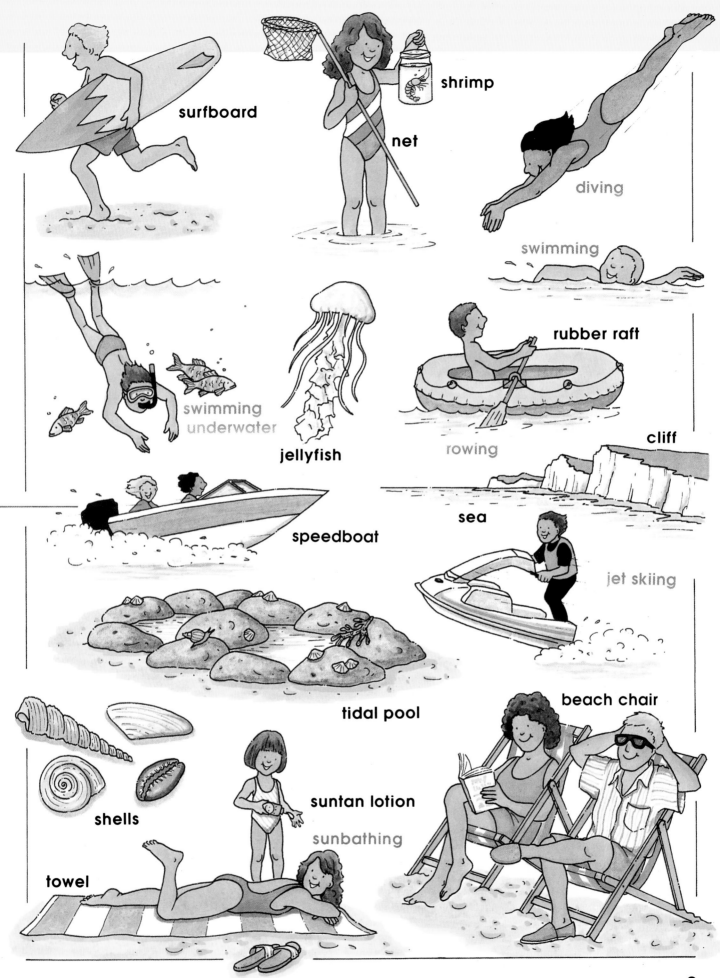

surfboard

shrimp

net

diving

swimming

swimming underwater

jellyfish

rubber raft

rowing

cliff

sea

speedboat

jet skiing

tidal pool

beach chair

shells

suntan lotion

sunbathing

towel

Buildings

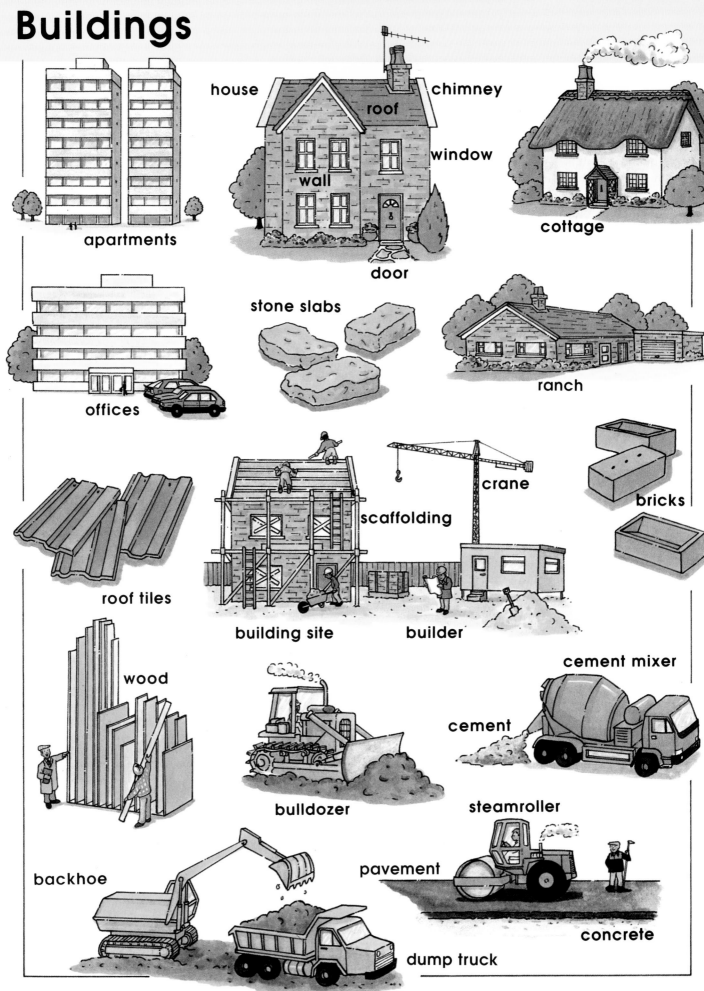

apartments

house

chimney

roof

window

wall

door

cottage

offices

stone slabs

ranch

roof tiles

scaffolding

crane

bricks

building site

builder

wood

cement mixer

cement

bulldozer

steamroller

backhoe

pavement

dump truck

concrete

On the move

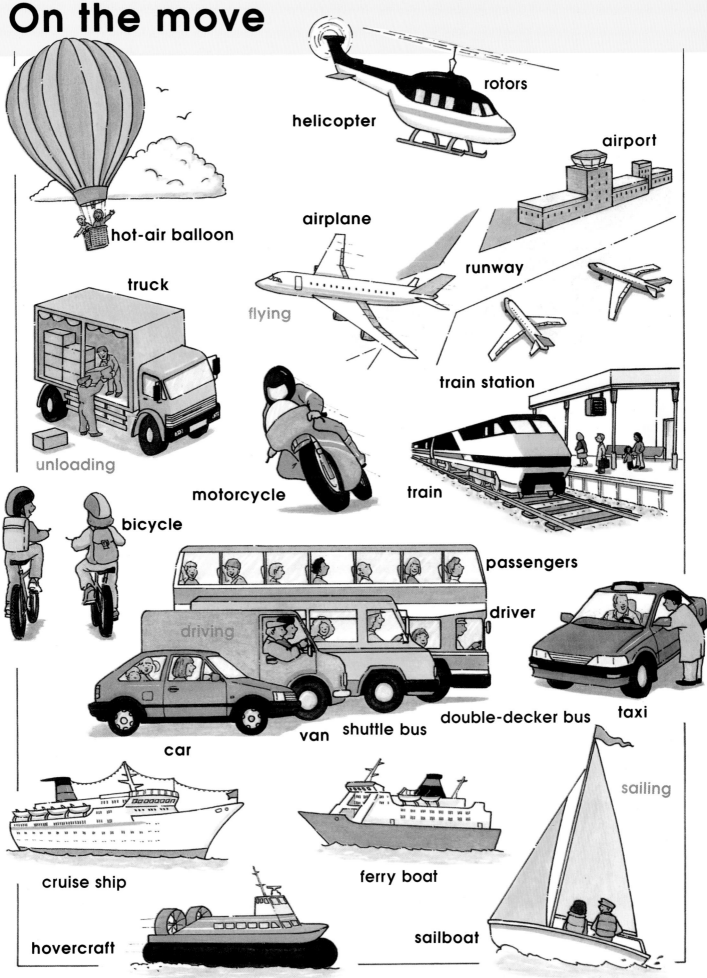

rotors

helicopter

airport

airplane

runway

flying

hot-air balloon

truck

train station

unloading

motorcycle

train

bicycle

passengers

driver

driving

double-decker bus

taxi

van   shuttle bus

car

sailing

cruise ship

ferry boat

hovercraft

sailboat

In the street

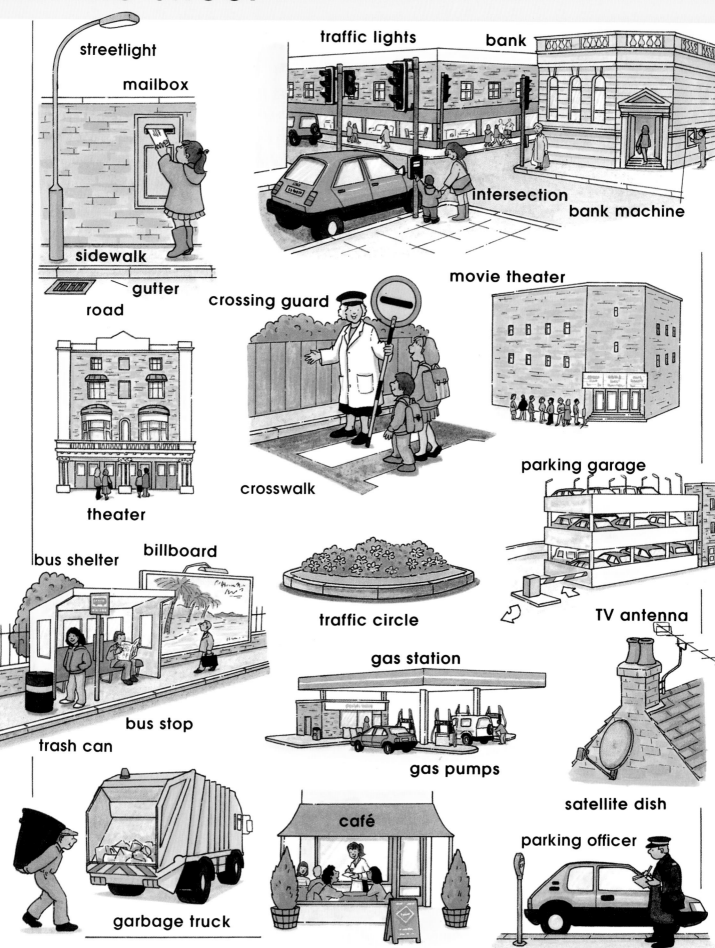

streetlight

mailbox

traffic lights

bank

intersection

bank machine

sidewalk

gutter

road

crossing guard

movie theater

theater

crosswalk

parking garage

bus shelter

billboard

traffic circle

TV antenna

gas station

bus stop

trash can

gas pumps

satellite dish

parking officer

garbage truck

café

12

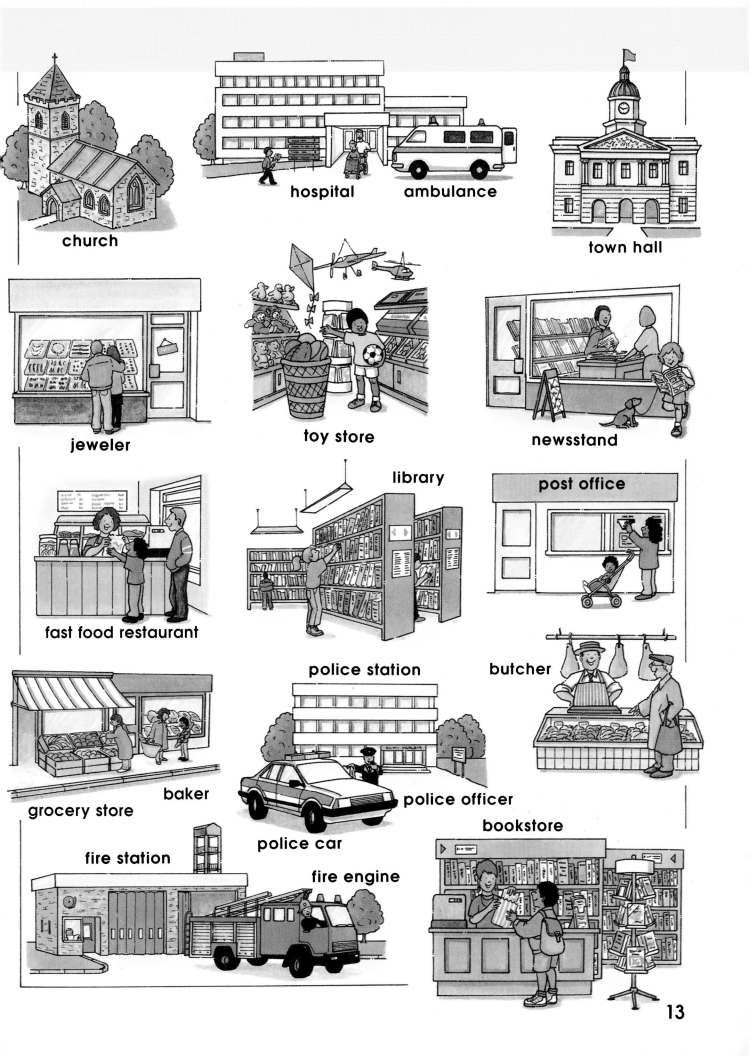

church

hospital　ambulance

town hall

jeweler

toy store

newsstand

fast food restaurant

library

post office

police station

butcher

grocery store

baker

police car

police officer

bookstore

fire station

fire engine

13

At the supermarket

shelves

rice and pasta

shopping cart

deli

fruit and vegetables

cashier

cash register

check-out

bar code

bakery

cream

yogurt

cheese

dairy foods

milk

money

receipt

household items

frozen food

label

canned goods

Cooking

wooden spoon

flour

powdered sugar

icing

stirring

mixing bowl

cookie sheet

recipe

pie

oven

tasting

cooking

ingredients

eggs

spatula

weighing

cookies

apron

scale

chopping

margarine

rolling

rolling pin

sugar

cookie cutter

At home

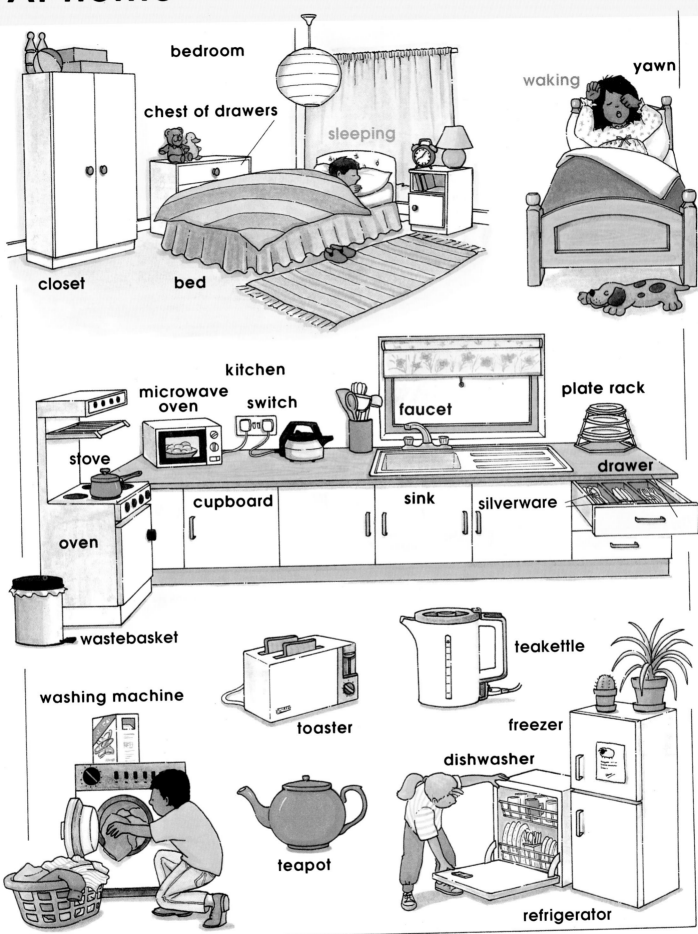

bedroom

chest of drawers

sleeping

waking   yawn

closet   bed

kitchen

microwave oven   switch   faucet   plate rack

stove

cupboard   sink   silverware   drawer

oven

wastebasket

washing machine

toaster

teakettle

freezer

dishwasher

teapot

refrigerator

mirror

brushing

bathroom

washing

soap

bubbles

sink

toilet

bath

upstairs

answering machine

front door

telephone

hall

downstairs

stereo

listening

armchair

living room

garage

shed

garden

watching

television

VCR

sofa

17

My family

young   younger   youngest

old   older   oldest

mommy   daddy

sister

brother

parents   son   daughter

uncle

aunt

nephew   niece

cousin

grandma

grandpa   grandchild

twins

baby

triplets

Party time

wrapping paper

birthday cards

presents

playing

Happy Birthday!

streamers

balloons

blowing

candles

birthday cake

happy

magician

prize

dancing

drinking

eating

full

About myself

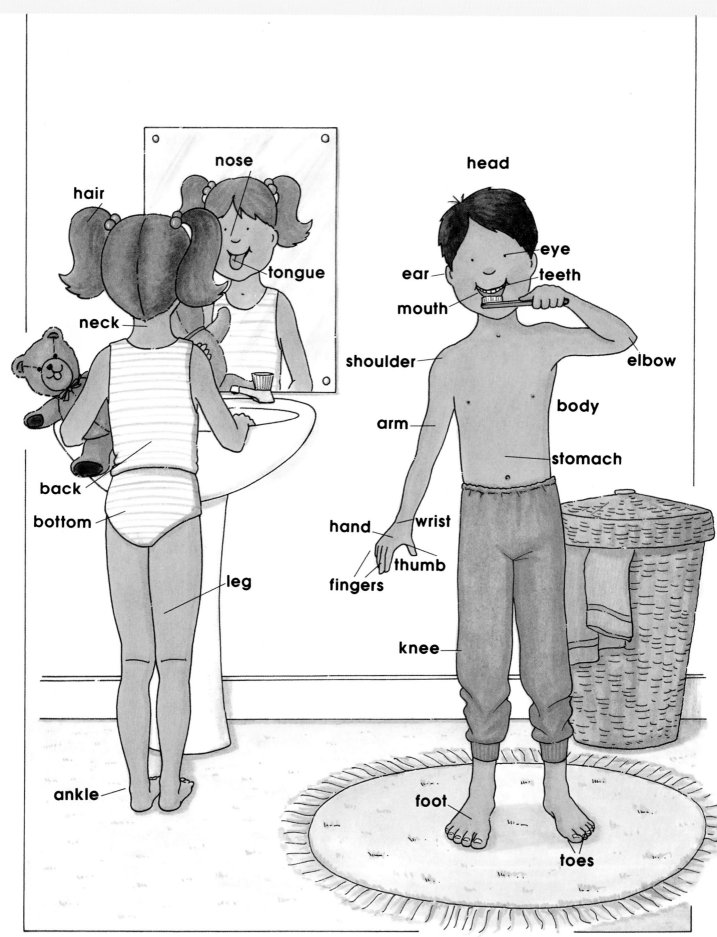

hair
nose
tongue
neck
back
bottom
leg
ankle

head
eye
ear
teeth
mouth
shoulder
elbow
body
arm
stomach
hand
wrist
thumb
fingers
knee
foot
toes

Feeling sick

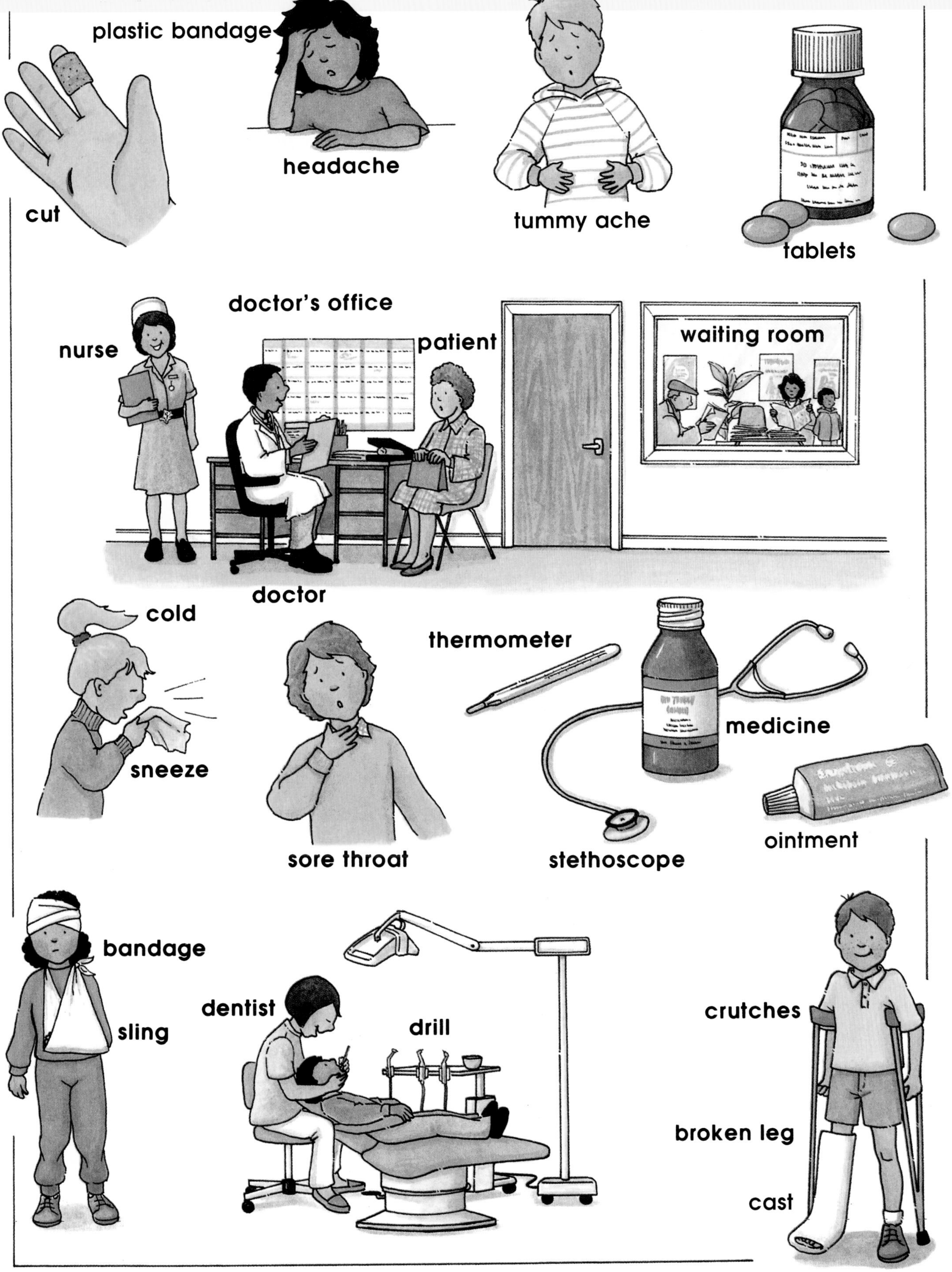

plastic bandage

headache

tummy ache

tablets

cut

nurse

doctor's office

patient

waiting room

doctor

cold

sneeze

thermometer

medicine

sore throat

stethoscope

ointment

bandage

dentist

drill

crutches

sling

broken leg

cast

Clothes

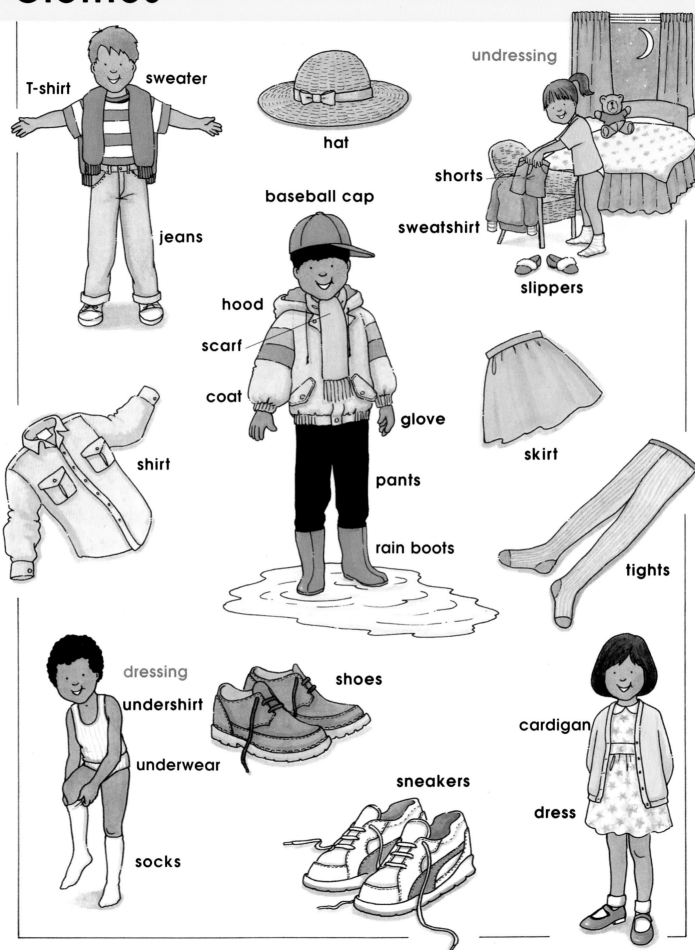

T-shirt

sweater

hat

baseball cap

undressing

shorts

sweatshirt

slippers

hood

scarf

coat

glove

pants

skirt

rain boots

tights

shirt

dressing

undershirt

underwear

socks

shoes

sneakers

cardigan

dress

22

Toys and games

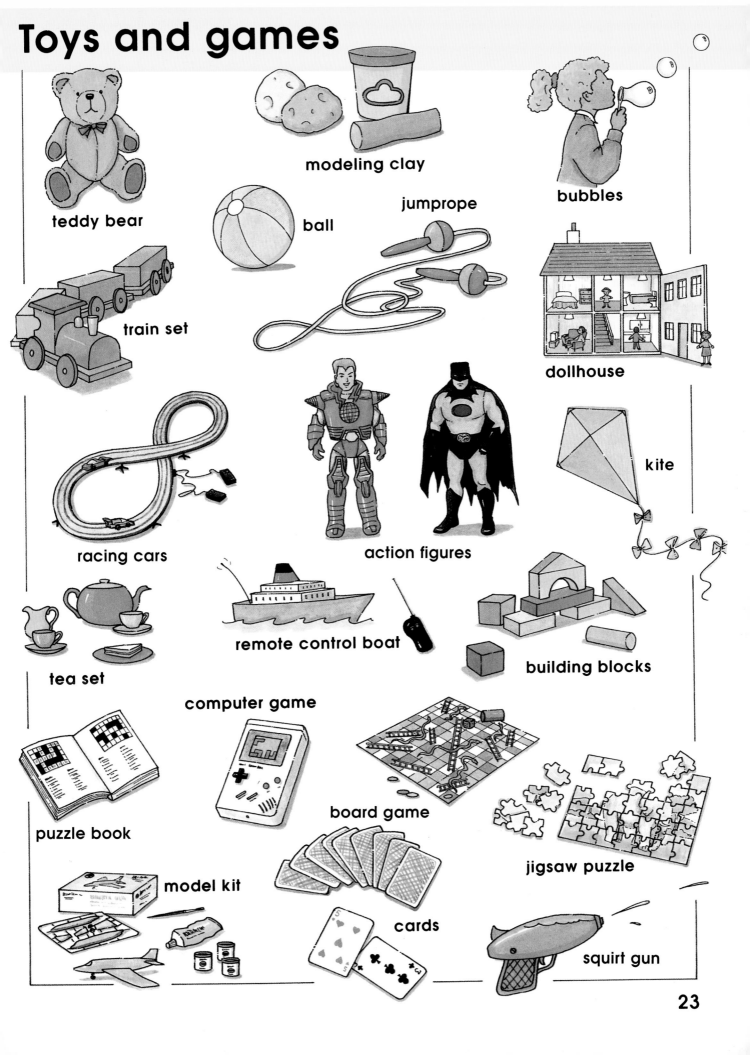

teddy bear

modeling clay

bubbles

ball

jumprope

train set

dollhouse

racing cars

action figures

kite

tea set

remote control boat

building blocks

computer game

puzzle book

board game

jigsaw puzzle

model kit

cards

squirt gun

At school

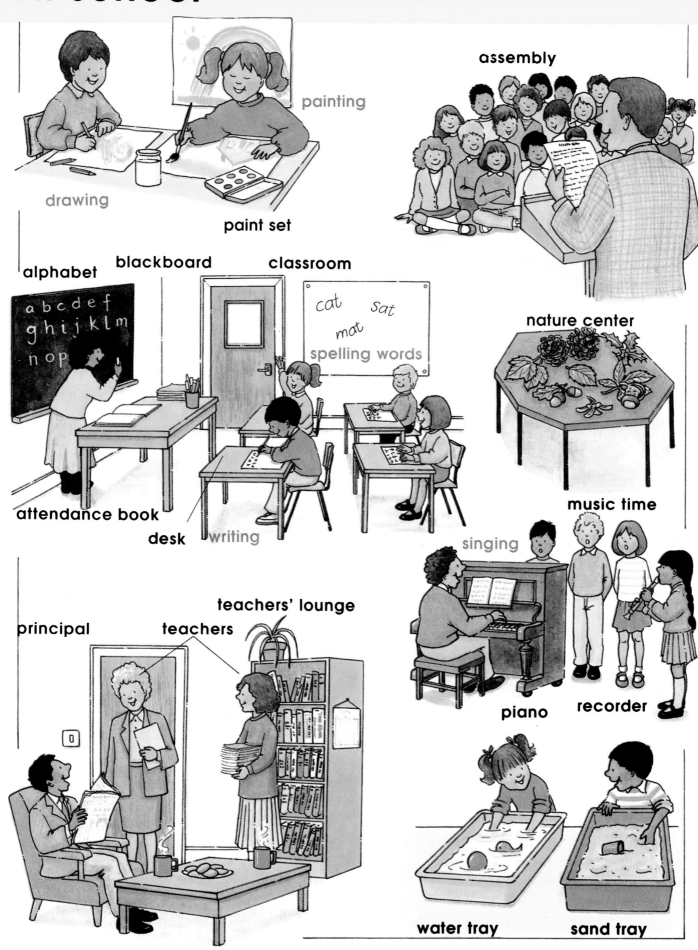

painting

drawing

paint set

assembly

alphabet

blackboard

classroom

cat sat mat
spelling words

nature center

attendance book

desk writing

music time

singing

teachers' lounge

principal   teachers

piano   recorder

water tray   sand tray

24

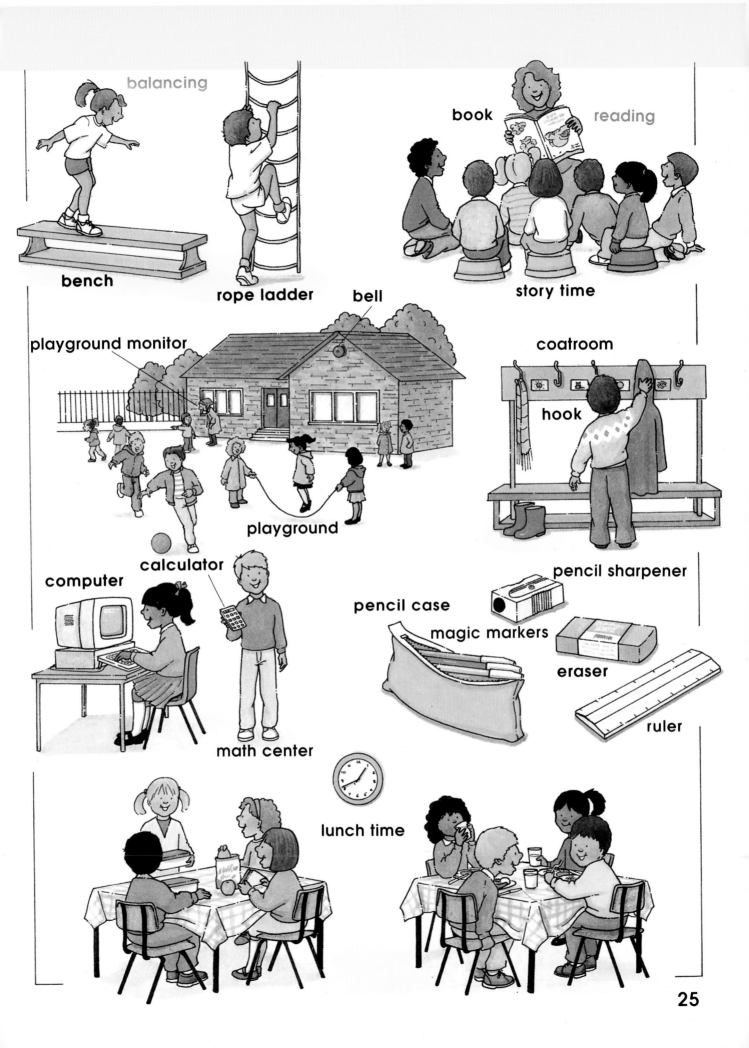

balancing

bench

rope ladder

bell

book

reading

story time

playground monitor

coatroom

hook

playground

calculator

computer

pencil sharpener

pencil case

magic markers

eraser

ruler

math center

lunch time

25

Shapes and colors

circle

semicircle

square

hexagon

triangle

rectangle

pentagon

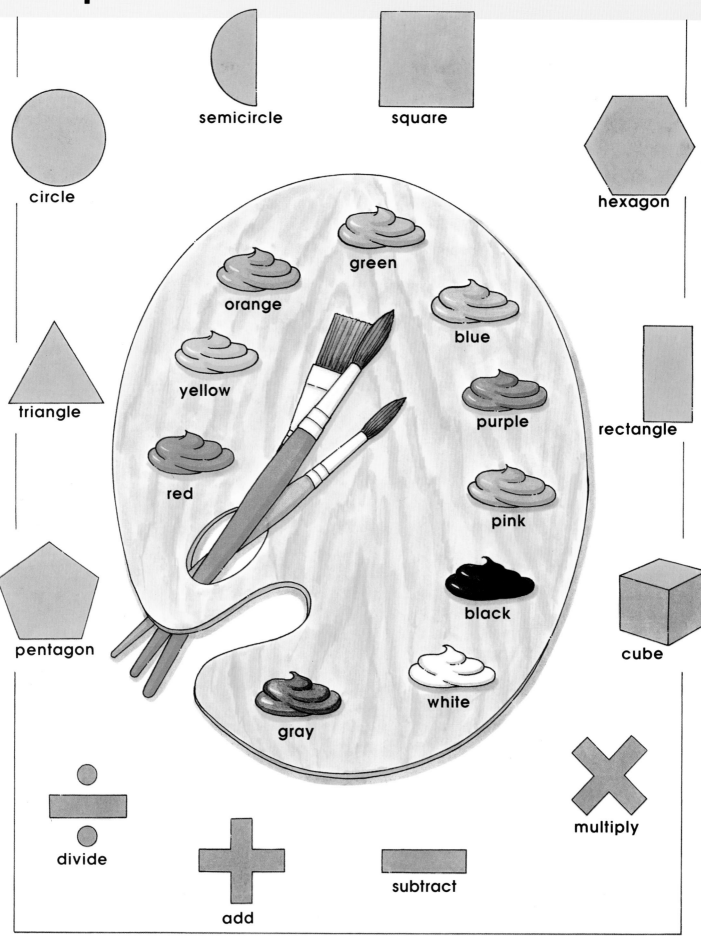

green

orange

blue

yellow

purple

red

pink

black

cube

white

gray

multiply

divide

add

subtract

26

Storytelling

elf

fairy

witch

kettle

palace

broom

toadstool

troll

pirate

treasure

cave

prince

princess

knight

King

Queen

throne

dragon

giant

monster

wizard

Our Earth

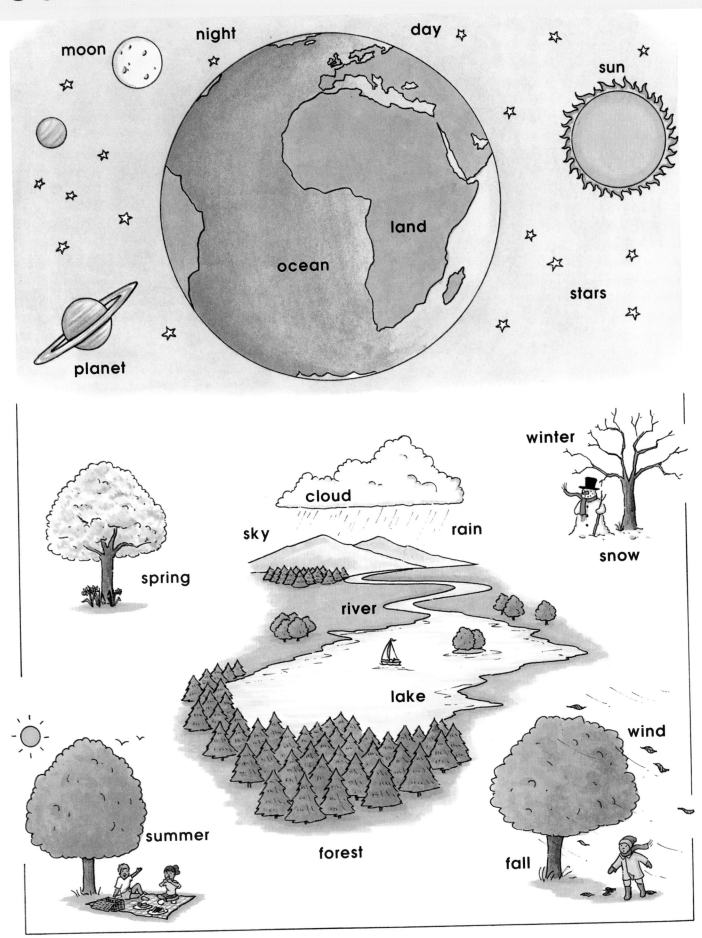

moon

night

day

sun

planet

ocean

land

stars

spring

cloud

sky

rain

winter

snow

river

lake

summer

forest

fall

wind

The words A-Z

The more difficult words are explained. This helps you learn what they mean and how to use them.

A

 action figures 23

 add 26

 airplane 11

 airport 11

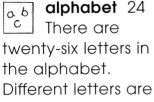 **alphabet** 24 There are twenty-six letters in the alphabet. Different letters are used to make different words.

 ambulance 13

 ankle 20

 answering machine 17 People can leave a message on this when you are not at home to answer the telephone.

 ant 3

 apartments 10

 apron 15

 arcade 7 A building where you can play videogames or other games.

 arm 20

 armchair 17

 assembly 24 The time when everybody in the school meets together.

 attendance book 24

 aunt 18

B

 baby 18

 back 20

 backhoe 10

 baker 13

 bakery 14

 balancing 25 Walking along steadily, so that you do not fall over.

 ball 23

 balloons 19

 bandage 21

 bank 12

 bank machine 12 A machine which gives you your money when you put in your bank card.

 bar code 14 A mark on things you buy. A computer reads it to find out the price.

 barn 5 A farm building used for storing things. Some farm animals, such as cows, live here.

 baseball cap 22

 basket 2

 basketball 6

 bat 6

 bath 17

 bathroom 17

 beach chair 9

 beach mat 8

 bed 16

 bedroom 16

 bee 3

 beehive 3 A house for bees. Honey is made here.

 beetle 3

 bell 25

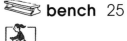 **bench** 25

 bicycle 11

 billboard 12

 birdseed 2

birthday cake 19

 birthday cards 19

 black 26

 blackboard 24

 blowing 19

 blue 26

 board game 23

 body 20

 bone 2

 book 25

 bookstore 13

 bottom 20

 bouncy castle 7

 bowl 2

 bowling game 8

 bricks 10

 broken leg 21

 broom 27

 brother 18

 brushing 17

 bubbles 17, 23

 bucket 8

 bug bottle 3
A bottle used for collecting and examining insects.

builder 10

 building blocks 23

building site 10

bull 5

bulldozer 10

bumper cars 7

bus shelter 12

bus stop 12

butcher 13

butterfly 3

C

 café 12

 cage 2

 calculator 25
A small machine that helps you work out math.

 camper 6

 campsite 6

 candles 19

 canned goods 14

 car 11

 cardigan 22

 cards 23

 cash register 14

 cashier 14

 cast 21

 cat 2

 catching 6

 caterpillar 3

 cave 27

 cement 10
Clay and sand mixed with water. It is used to stick bricks and stone together.

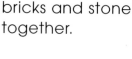 **cement mixer** 10

 check-out 14

 cheese 14

 cheetah 4
A very large spotted member of the cat family. It can run extremely fast.

 chest of drawers 16

 chimney 10

 chopping 15

 church 13

 circle 26
A round shape.

 classroom 24

cliff 9
Where the edge of the land goes down very steeply to meet the sea.

 climbing 6

 closet 16

 cloud 28

 coat 22

 coatroom 25

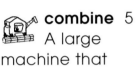 **cold** 21

 combine 5
A large machine that farmers use to cut down and collect their crops.

 computer 25

 **computer game** 23

 concrete 10
Cement, gravel and sand mixed with water. It is used to make roads and floors.

 cookie cutter 15

 cookie sheet 15

 cookies 15

 cooking 15

 cottage 10
A small house, maybe in the country.

 cotton candy 7

 **cousin** 18
Your aunt's or uncle's son or daughter.

 cow 5

 crab 8

 crane 10

 crawling 3

 cream 14

 crocodile 4
An animal like a large lizard which lives in the waters of tropical countries.

 crossing guard 12

 crosswalk 12
A safe place to cross the road.

 cruise ship 11

 crutches 21

 cube 26
A square block.

 cupboard 16

 cut 21

D

 daddy 18

 dairy foods 14

 dancing 19

 daughter 18

 day 28

 deli 14
A store, or a counter in a store, which sells special kinds of cheeses and cooked meats.

 dentist 21

 desk 24

 digging 8

 dishwasher 16

 divide 26

 diving 9

 doctor 21

 doctor's office 21

 dog 2

 doghouse 2

 dollhouse 23

 dolphin 4

 door 10

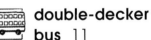 **double-decker bus** 11

 downstairs 17

 dragon 27

 drawer 16

 drawing 24

 dress 22

 dressing 22

drill 21

 drinking 19

 driver 11

 driving 11

 duck 5

 duck pond 5

 dump truck 10

E

 ear 20

 earth 3

 eating 19

 eel 4
A fish that is shaped like a snake.

 eggs 15

 elbow 20

 elephant 4

 elf 27

 eraser 25

 eye 20

F

 fairy 27

 fall 28
The season when the days become shorter and colder. Fall comes before winter.

 farm 5

 farmer 5

 fast-food restaurant 13

 faucet 16

 ferris wheel 7

 ferry boat 11
A boat that carries people or cars across rivers or seas.

 field 5

 fingers 20

 fire engine 13

 fire station 13

 fish 2

 fish bowl 2

 fish food 2

 fishing net 3

 flippers 8

 flour 15

 fly 3

 flying 11

 foot 20

 forest 28

 freezer 16

 french fries 7

 frog 3

 front door 17

 frozen food 14
Food stored in the freezer so that it stays fresh for a long time.

 fruit 14

 full 19

G

 garage 17

 garbage truck 12

 garden 17

 gas pumps 12

 gas station 12

 gate 5

 gerbil 2

 giant 27

 giraffe 4

 glove 22

 go-carts 7

 goggles 8
Plastic glasses you wear when you are swimming to keep the water out of your eyes.

 goose 5

 gorilla 4

 grandchild 18

32

grandma 18

 grandpa 18

 gray 26

 green 26

 grocery store 13

 guinea pig 2

 gutter 12
A grate along the side of the road that carries rain water away and down a drain.

H

 hair 20

 hall 17

 hamburger 7

 hamster 2

 hand 20

 happy 19

 Happy Birthday! 19

 hat 22

 haunted house 7

 head 20

 headache 21

 hedge 5

 helicopter 11

 helmet 6

 hen 5

 hexagon 26
A shape with six sides.

 hill 5

 hippopotamus 4

 holding 2

 hood 22

 hook 25

 horse 5

 hospital 13

 hot air balloon 11

 hot dog 7

 house 10

 household items 14

 hovercraft 11
A boat that floats on a cushion of air over land or water. It normally carries passengers.

 hutch 2

I

 ice cream 8

 ice cream stand 8
A small store where ice cream is sold.

 icing 15

 ingredients 15
The different foods you need when you are cooking, such as vegetables or meat.

 inner tube 8

 intersection 12

J

 jeans 22

jellyfish 9

jet skiing 9

jeweler 13

jigsaw puzzle 23

jumping rope 6

jumprope 23

K

kangaroo 4

kettle 27
A big pot used for cooking.

kicking 6

King 27

kitchen 16

 kite 23

 kitten 2

 knee 20

 knight 27

L

 label 14

 lake 28

 lamb 5

land 28

 leg 20

 library 13

 lifeguard 8
Somebody who helps swimmers who are in trouble.

 line 7

 lion 4

listening 17

 living room 17

M

 magic markers 25

 magician 19

 magnifying glass 3

 mailbox 12

 making 8

 margarine 15

 math center 25

 maze 7

 medicine 21
Syrup or tablets that a doctor or parent gives you when you are sick.

 merry-go-round 7

 microwave oven 16
A small oven that cooks food very quickly.

 milk 14

 mirror 17

 mixing bowl 15

 moat 8
A ditch that is built around the edge of a castle and is filled with water.

 model kit 23

 modeling clay 23

 mommy 18

 money 14

 monkey 4

 monkey bars 6

 monster 27

 moon 28

 moth 3

 motorcycle 11

 mouse 2

 mouth 20

 movie theater 12

 multiply 26

 music time 24

N

 nature center 24

 neck 20

 nephew 18
If you are a boy, your aunt and uncle will call you their nephew.

 nest 3

 net 9

 newsstand 13

 niece 18
If you are a girl, your aunt and uncle will call you their niece.

 night 28

 nose 20

 nurse 21

O

 ocean 28
A very large area of sea, for example, the Atlantic or Pacific Ocean.

 octopus 4

 **offices** 10

 **ointment** 21
You can put this on a cut or scrape to help kill any bad germs.

 **old** 18

 older 18

 oldest 18

 orange 26

 **orchard** 5
A field planted with fruit trees.

 oven 15, 16

P

 pads 6

 paint set 24

 painting 24

 palace 27

 pants 22

 parakeet 2

 parents 18

 parking garage 12

 parking officer 12
Somebody who makes sure that cars are parked in the right places.

 passengers 11

 pasta 14
A type of Italian food made from flour.

 patient 21

 pavement 10

 pebbles 8
Little stones.

 pencil case 25

 pencil sharpener 25

 penguin 4

 pentagon 26
A shape with five sides.

 perch 2

 petting 2

 piano 24

 picnic 6

 pie 15

 pier 8
A structure which stands on legs, and which leads out over the water. It might have a café or amusement park on it.

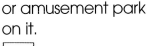 **pig** 5

 pigpen 5
Fenced area where pigs live.

 pill bug 3
An insect which lives in rotten wood and which can curl up into a ball when it is in danger.

 pink 26

 pirate 27

 planet 28
Earth is one of the nine planets which go around the Sun.

 plastic bandage 21

 plate rack 16

 playground 6, 25
Where children can play on things such as swings or rope ladders.

 playground monitor 25

 playing 19

 polar bear 4

 police car 13

 police officer 13

 police station 13

 pond 3

 pool 4

popcorn 7

 post office 13

 powdered sugar 15

 presents 19

 prince 27

 princess 27

 principal 24

 prize 19
A present you are given when you win a competition.

 puppy 2

 purple 26

 puzzle book 23

Q

 Queen 27

R

 rabbit 2

 racing cars 23

 rain 28

 rain boots 22

 ramp 6
A slope. Skateboarders use a specially-made ramp to speed up and down on.

 ranch 10
A house which does not have an upstairs.

 reading 25

 receipt 14
A piece of paper which shows how much you have spent.

 recipe 15
This tells you what ingredients you need and how to mix them when you are cooking.

 recorder 24

 rectangle 26
A shape with four sides and four corners.

 **red** 26

 refrigerator 16

 remote control boat 23

 rhinoceros 4

 rice 14

 riding 7

 river 28

 road 12

 rollerskates 6

 roller coaster 7
A ride at an amusement park where the cars speed along a track which goes up and down.

 rolling 15

 rolling pin 15

 roof 10

 roof tiles 10

 rope ladder 25

 ropes 6

 rotors 11

 rowing 9

 rubber raft 9

 ruler 25

 running 4

 runway 11
A long flat road from which airplanes gather speed and take off.

S

 sailboat 11

 sailing 11

 sand 8

 sand tray 24

 sandcastle 8

satellite dish 12
A large metal dish on the side of a house. It picks up television programs which have been broadcast from far away.

 scaffolding 10
Poles which are bolted together for builders to climb when they are working on high buildings.

 scale 15
These measure how heavy things are.

 scarf 22

 scratching 4

 screaming 7

 sea 9

 seal 4

 seaweed 8

 semicircle 26
Half a circle.

 shark 4

 shed 17

 sheep 5

 shells 9

 shelves 14

 shirt 22

 shoes 22

 shopping cart 14

 shorts 22

 shoulder 20

 shovel 8

 shrimp 9
A small animal that lives in the sea.

 shuttle bus 11

 sidewalk 12
Path which runs along the side of the road.

 silverware 16

 singing 24

 sink 16, 17

 sister 18

 skateboard 6

 skirt 22

 sky 28

 sleeping 16

 slide 6, 7

 sling 21

 slippers 22

 snake 4

 sneakers 22

 sneeze 21

 snorkel 8
A plastic tube that you can breathe through when you swim just below the surface of the water.

 snow 28

 soap 17

 soccer 6

 socks 22

 sofa 17

 son 18

 sore throat 21

 spatula 15
A wide, blunt knife used for cooking.

 speedboat 9

 spelling words 24
A list of words to learn to spell.

 spider 3

 splashing 6

 spring 28
The season when the days become longer and warmer. Plants start to grow new leaves again.

 square 26
A shape with four sides all the same length.

 squirt gun 23

 stable 5
A building where horses live.

 starfish 8

 stars 28

steamroller 10

 stereo 17

 stethoscope 21
A doctor uses this to listen to your breathing.

 stirring 15

 stomach 20

 stone slabs 10

 story time 25

 stove 16

 straw 2
Dried stalks of plants used to keep animals warm.

 stream 5

 streamers 19
Colorful strips of paper to decorate a room with when you have a party.

 streetlight 12

 subtract 26

 sugar 15

 summer 28
The season when the days are long and warm.

 sun 28

 sunbathing 9

 suntan lotion 9

 surfboard 9

 swarm 3
A lot of bees or other insects flying together in a group.

 sweater 22

 sweatshirt 22

 swimming 9

 swimming underwater 9

 swings 6

 switch 16

T

 tablets 21
The doctor gives you these when you are ill.

 tasting 15

 taxi 11

 teakettle 16

 tea set 23

 teachers 24

 teachers' lounge 24

 teapot 16

 teddy bear 23

 teeth 20

 telephone 17

 television 17

 tent 6

 theater 12
A building where people go to see ballets, shows, or plays.

 thermometer 21
This measures how hot something is. Doctors use a thermometer to measure your temperature.

 throne 27

 throwing 6

 thumb 20

 tidal pool 9

 tiger 4

 tights 22

 toadstool 27
A fungus like a mushroom. It can be poisonous.

 toaster 16

 toes 20

 toilet 17

 tongue 20

 towel 9

 town hall 13
Where important decisions about the town are made.

toy store 13

 tractor 5

 traffic circle 12
A circle where several roads meet.

 traffic lights 12

 train 11

 train set 23

 train station 11

 trash can 12

 treasure 27

 triangle 26
A shape with three sides.

 triplets 18
Three children born together at the same time from the same mother.

 troll 27
A monster that only exists in fairy tales.

 truck 5, 11

 T-shirt 22

 tummy ache 21

 turtle 4
Looks a little like a tortoise. It has flipper-shaped legs and can swim underwater.

 TV antenna 12
This makes the picture on your television clear.

 twins 18
Two children born together at the same time from the same mother.

U

 uncle 18

 undershirt 22

 underwear 22

 undressing 22

 unloading 11
When you take objects out of something, for example, boxes out of a truck.

 upstairs 17

V

 van 11

 VCR 17

 vegetables 14

W

 wading 8

 wading pool 6

 waiting room 21

 waking 16

 wall 10

 washing 17

 washing machine 16

 wasp 3

 wastebasket 16

 watching 17

 water bottle 2

 water slide 7
A ride at a theme park. People sit in boats which shoot along open chutes of water.

 water fight 6

 water skiing 8

 water tray 24

 water wings 8
You wear these on your arms to help you float in the water.

 web 3
Spiders make webs to trap flies in.

 weighing 15

 wet suit 8
This is made of rubber. You wear it in the water to keep you warm.

 white 26

 wind 28

 window 10

wings 3

winter 28
The season when the days are short and cold.

 witch 27
An ugly old woman who casts bad spells.

 wizard 27
An old man who has magic powers.

 woods 5
A group of trees.

 wood 10
Trees can be cut up into planks of wood and used to make furniture or other things.

 wood shavings 2
Fine wood shavings which are used to keep pets in cages clean and dry.

 wooden spoon 15

 worm 3

 wrapping paper 19

 wrist 20

 writing 24

Y

 yawn 16

 yellow 26

 yogurt 14

 young 18

 younger 18

 youngest 18

Z

 zebra 4

This book was created by Zigzag, a division of Chrysalis Books Limited, 10, Blenheim Court, Brewery Road, London N7 9NT, U.K. A member of the Chrysalis Group plc.

Design: Chris Leishman:
Series concept: Tony Potter
Color separations: Studiotech Ltd., Leeds, England
Printed in India

Published in the U.S. by McGraw-Hill Children's Publishing, 8787 Orion Place, Columbus, OH 43240. Previously distributed in the U. S. by Smithmark Publishers.

This edition © 1997, 2000 by Zigzag Publishing and Chrysalis Books Limited

8020

ISBN 1-57768-780-9

McGraw-Hill
Children's Publishing
A Division of The McGraw-Hill Companies